Our Central Command Post: An Adaptive Military Family Home

JEANNETTE DAVIDSON-MAYER

DEDICATION

To My Love and to My Daughter who have grown stronger together in the face of adversity. I truly could not have made it without either of you.

To Our Military Families who proudly serve our Country in time of War and Peace, and continually live with the long-term side effects of war.

To our Hidden Heroes who support our Veterans through the long-term side effects of war. These Mothers, Fathers, Spouses, Siblings, and Friends are truly blessings, Angels on Earth. Our Hidden Heroes show true love and dedication to those who gave all. Visit www.hiddenheroes.org or www.elizabethdolefoundation.org.

To R4 Alliance which is paving a new pathway in saving the lives of Our Military Family through Recreational Therapy. Those small successes in recreational therapy can be carried over into everyday life, bringing people out of darkness. Before the publishing of this book, R4 Alliance has been purchased by American Warriors Partnership creating a greater resource for Recreational programs.

CONTENTS

ACKNOWLEDGMENTS

Thank you to My Love, aka DeWayne Mayer, for his years of dedication to our marriage. For his never giving up through all my crazy ideas of creating a functional/non-functional, adaptive home that works with our ever-changing, daily new normal.

Thank you to our loving daughter Addy Mayer who has grown up learning right alongside her daddy. So many times Addy has been the secondary caregiver, robbing her of childhood at times. Addy did so with a smile because her Daddy remains her hero.

To the Elizabeth Dole Foundation, which has shown me that there are so many fellow Hidden Heroes who share similar struggles. They have opened my eyes to new friendships, new-found strengths, and new resources to keep moving forward. Most of all, that as a Hidden Hero, we are Not Alone!

To R4 Alliance which continues to pave this pathway to link well-vetted recreational therapy programs together creating a stronger network Nationwide in supporting Our Military Families. Bringing them up out of darkness, leading them towards success, while saving lives. Because taking care of Our Military Families doesn't fall on our government; it falls on all of us as Civilians pulling together for a greater a cause.

TESTIMONIALS

"Our military caregivers are the unsung heroes of our nation's wars and readiness, and Jeannette poignantly highlights some of the significant challenges they face on a daily basis. At the same time, she embodies the hopeful and optimistic spirit of so many of our "Hidden Heroes." Our Central Command Post should be required reading for all of our nation's leaders so they can truly understand the repercussions of war what a "new normal" really means."

~ Justin Constantine, Justin Constantine Group

"Jeanette's monograph is Olympic. By weaving her continuing efforts to care for Dewayne, her family and herself, the value systems of Commitment, Dedication, Sacrifice, Persistence and Perseverations come into full display. This is a must read for anyone who chooses to be inspired by one family's mission to care of a loved one. A must read for any caregiver whatever the disability or leaders who cares for their charge."

~ Chip Fisher Chairman/CEO R4 Alliance.

"Watching my sister and brother-in-law go through the trials associated with injuries sustained in war has been simultaneously heartbreaking and awe-inspiring. My brother-in-law is a kind, loving man who used to be a physically active, hardworking, member of the family. Now he is still kind and loving, but he cannot be physically active nor work hard. It is heartbreaking to watch him sit on the sidelines of life. My sister has always been clever. She is blessed with an ability to think outside the box. She has done a lot of thinking in the past few years! Her adaptive-minded approach to life has improved her family's situation and allowed her husband to participate in life to the extent possible.. I have used some of her suggestions in my own life. I am very proud of my sister for writing this book. I am also proud of her for standing by her husband through all the hard times. It is my hope that this book will help someone else in a similar situation.

~ Anne Davidson Moscrip, Jeannette's sister

"Our Central Command Post is a must read for new caregivers, seasoned caregivers, and people who are interested in understanding what it means when the war comes home with the soldier. It is a poignant, thoughtful, and provocative read. Jeannette gently brings us into the fold of her new normal and how it continues to change. It is an honor to serve with Jeannette as a 2016-2018 Elizabeth Dole Fellow. This read will not disappoint."

~Mary Hahn Ward, Advocate, Educator, Photographer, Writer

PREFACE

Some people may think an adaptive home is only needed for those who have a physical disability. For a person who is in a wheelchair or has an amputation, you can plainly see what challenges the person might be facing. Their injuries are clearly seen.

There are injuries that aren't clearly seen. Injuries that many of our veterans live with. Some of us caregivers call these, "Side effects of War." It was brought to my attention that there isn't a clear understanding of why adaptations are needed for cognitive disabilities. Cognitive disabilities are not something generally thought about. They are definitely visible. But when you live with a person who has a traumatic brain injury that continually worsens, you learn how to adapt. For their cognitive abilities are part of an ever-changing, daily new normal that require adaptations in a home. These adaptations help support this person's everyday life. The adaptations become necessary for that person to have some level of successful functionality.

With these adaptations we have to be flexible. Why? Because cognitive disabilities do not stay consistent. They continually change. As they change, so do the adaptations. This book is to support all those caregivers living with someone who has cognitive challenges. The ideas/suggestions in this book are just that: ideas/suggestions. They are adjustable to fit the needs of your home.

Make notes in this book. Journal. Take time to work through your thoughts and emotions as you work through your journey.

Know you are not alone. Find a caregiver partner, a counselor, a friend to help support you through this process.

Never second guess yourself. Believe in yourself for you truly know what is right for your home.

CH 1: IT'S OKAY

Not everyone has the strength or character to live the "caregiver life"....
to hold on for the long haul when your world feels out of control. Not
holding on is okay. No Judgments. Promise.

Not holding on doesn't make you any less or any more of a person, it
just means this lifestyle wasn't something meant for you.

It also shows that we can't hold onto the past, nor can we recreate the
past. We can only learn how to let go of the past the best we can so we can
move forward, and grab a hold of the future we have been dealt. My hope
for you reading this book is to find the inner strength needed to keep
moving forward in a direction that you need to go, and to create the home
environment needed to support you in your journey.

A counselor once told me I have to literally bury the husband I married
(in my mind) so I could learn to accept the man who came home from war.
I thought she was crazy until I read Bob and Lee Woodruff's book, In An
Instant.

Lee shared this same process of mentally "burying" her pre-combat-
zone husband. This allowed her to break free of trying to make him return
back to his former self because he was forever changed.

When I heard two professional people sharing the same view point, I
knew it was time for me to stop being stubborn and start looking into this
process. I knew in my heart that we couldn't move forward as a family if I
was still holding onto what would never be.

Bob and Lee's book was a great place to start in my journey. Learning
about their journey gave me strength and the hope that one day I would be
able to create my own successful journey. Over the next several months, I
began our new journey, which started with me. I continued to read through

their book, attended my counseling sessions, and tagged along with my husband to his many, many medical appointments.

One day it hit me!

I could be in control of this journey. It was time to take our life -- which now felt so out-of-control -- and grab ahold of it, so we could direct the outcomes. We finally had control over the journey.

By August 21, 2008, I finished reading Bob and Lee's book. Filled with sticky tabs, underlining, and journal pages, my last entry in the back of the book read, "Finally finished the book. Feelings of hope and despair occupy my mind. Overwhelmed with all I have read. One day I pray for the acceptance and peace for My Love's Traumatic Brain Injury." This monumental day of acceptance came and went with no fanfare. But it came. Living with a hubby that has a TBI is now easier most days.

This path of burying (in my mind) the man I married was painful. In the end it brought clarity with peace and acceptance. Once I reached this new level of understanding our lives became manageable once more. I was able to learn to accept what we could change while living with the ever-changing daily new normal that Traumatic Brain Injury (TBI) and Post Traumatic Stress Disorder (PTSD) throw at us. Now keep in mind, I am human, which means there are days where I forget to breathe, I forget to keep the man I married buried (in my mind).

There are times I really miss what we had, and what our dreams were. It takes some rebuilding to get back on track to focus back to who we are now, but I get there. I remind myself it is OK to get angry, angry at the TBI, angry at the PTSD - but try really hard to not angry at the man.

It is that separation of the man, the person, from the ailments that helps me cope. I work through the anger to focus on what needs to be changed to meet his new normal. Then remind myself that change is going to be a constant in our home, in our lives, and that is okay!

As you will learn later on in the book, the power of sticky notes came in handy, not only for My Love's ever-changing daily new normal but they also came in handy to support our family's mental wellbeing. They've truly become a family support need.

Keep in mind, our life was and continues to be, a challenge. In the beginning there were many times I was ready to walk away because I didn't feel I could take the chaos any longer. Then I would look at our daughter, remember the joyful moments, cry, pray, scream, then try to remember to reach out for more help so we could keep it together. A little trick I learned was to cry in the shower. This was a safe place to keep the tears hidden from my family so not to add more stress to their day. It works to help wash away the tears, the stress, to start out refreshed.

Now for the really hard part to admit and might be a tad challenging for some readers. There are times I have to be the one literally turning off the

TV while forcing My Love off the couch to take Ava (the service dog) for a walk or get ready to leave. At times DeWayne has to be given only choice A or B in order to help simplify his thinking process. This also help keep him from less "squirrel moments."

We have learned over the years how to determine when DeWayne requires direct conversation and at what level. This way, he can be a part of family, making decisions successfully.

When it comes to secure access for our financial information and other valuable information, DeWayne has limited access to prevent him from overspending or placing our personal information at risk. With his TBI, his critical thinking skills operate at a lower level skill rate and he has jeopardized our information multiple times in the past. Not a risk I am willing to take any longer.

To prevent this from reoccurring, the best option was to limit his access. At times it does, sadly, feel like I am having to treat DeWayne like a child. I don't want to treat my husband this way and for both of us, it causes mental distress and heartache. I know I have grown a bit callous over the years to some of the behaviors that occur in our home, but I also know that keeping my husband safe, keeping our financial and personal information safe, and accepting that my husband requires this lower level skill management works.

Do I love it? Heck no!

Reflection Point
Use the notes pages in this book to think through the key points of each chapter. Your journey may not be exactly like mine, but I found it therapeutic to journal as I went through this transition to our new normal.

- Has there ever been a time when you have felt like you didn't feel that everything was okay?

- How could you think through the situation to figure out what would make it easier or help you get through it?

Notes

_____
_____
_____
_____
_____
_____
_____
_____
_____
_____
_____
_____
_____
_____
_____
_____
_____
_____
_____
_____
_____
_____

CH 2: THE THINKING ENDED

We knew DeWayne's deployment was going to create changes in our family. We knew there was a chance that he would come home either uninjured, injured or dead. That was the end of my thinking on the possibilities of changes to our family. DeWayne left for training July 2004 stateside. Followed by being in Iraq by December 2004.

May 23, 2005, the Family Support Team received notification of the death of SSG John Ogburn "Oggie". I can remember the Major pulling me aside to let me know that my husband was in the humvee with Oggie at the time of the accident but there was not medical report at that time on him. My brain still did not fully engage that change was coming home and that change was occurring at home.

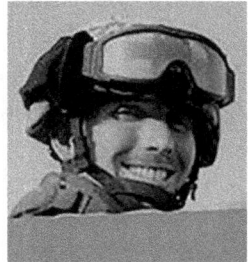

October 2, 2005 -- actually with the time zone changes that would have made it October 1, 2005 for me -- I felt extremely tired with body aches, felt similar to the flu yet eerily different. By midnight I was finally able to close my eyes only to be woken up a few hours later with the phone ringing.

Looking at the caller ID, I knew it was someone from Iraq calling. I didn't want to answer the phone. The irrational part of my brain knew if I didn't answer, then "it" didn't happen. But the rational part knew, if I didn't answer the phone this could lead to people showing up on my doorstep.

So, I answered the phone.

My husband's commanding officer did a fine job reporting to me what he knew at that moment. I allowed the irrational brain to take over again explaining this wasn't notification protocol. The officer politely explained why he broke protocol and nudged me in the right direction. Before the officer hung up, he told me he would be calling back as soon as he knew anything.

5

October 2nd was the end of our old family life as we knew it.

Because it felt so far away, my brain still hadn't processed the change. All I could think about was getting my husband home. I was done with hearing the mortar attacks while on the phone with him. I was done with occasional phone calls, letters or emails. It was time for us to be a family again.

DeWayne came home mid-October 2005 on the advance plane from Iraq. He was sent to Madigan Army Medical Center in Tacoma, WA, to start his medical evaluations. By February 2006, DeWayne was sent home placed in a home-based health care program through the Army. Over a year later DeWayne was placed on the Temporary Disabled Retirement List through the Army, where his medical care was transferred to the Boise VA Medical Center.

It wasn't until my husband was going through his VA medical enrollment that I learned of the other three "close calls" that contributed to his moderate to severe Traumatic Brain Injury (TBI) and Post Traumatic Stress Disorder (PTSD).

Living with the side effects of war kind of snuck up on us. The excitement of having DeWayne home truly covered up many complications. Missed medical appointments, misunderstandings of what doctors were telling him, forgetting what was said during his medical appointment, frustration mounting at home, and the excitement of "Dad" being home, soon wore off as the anger took over.

This is when the process began, and our ever changing adaptive home was born.

Reflection Point

Use the notes pages in this book to think through the key points of each chapter. Your journey may not be exactly like mine, but I found it therapeutic to journal as I went through this transition to our new normal.

- Have you experienced the shock of unexpected news?

- How did the news affect you?

- What are/were your initial feelings around this news?

Notes

JEANNETTE DAVIDSON-MAYER

CH 3: "OUR CENTRAL COMMAND POST," COMMONLY KNOWN TO MOST AS "THE KITCHEN"

By the time the command post was born, we had reached our functioning limitations as people, and as a family. Creating order out of disorder was mandatory, and we knew we had to create space and systems my husband could use (and so could we).

It was time to centralize the chaos. Our home life was spiraling out of control. We were playing hide-n-seek with car keys, my hubby's wallet, glasses, hearing aids, dishes, jackets, remote controls (literally found in rooms the TV was not) and so on. Keeping track of our family schedule was not happening. This chaos was no longer enjoyable. Jokes and laughter could no longer be created. Demise of the family unit was inevitable.

Drastic measures began.

First, we worked closely with DeWayne's occupational therapist at the VA. We tried many different modalities. We tried different notebooks to track things, binders with dividers, task sheets, and schedule pages on the computer. We set alarms on his phone, bought him a Personal Digital Assistant (PDA), and a small calendar whiteboard. All great planning ideas but none worked.

My brain was aching to discover something that would support My Love to be successful in his daily living. We even tried the big orange brain book. The modalities options were endless. Some we quickly scrapped and others became lifesavers. The keepers became an adventure because they required fine-tuning to meet my hubby's needs as his new normal changed daily!

The Keepers

Our first step to create organized chaos was to centralize it. Here is where we centralized everything to our kitchen. We figured, who doesn't find comfort in the kitchen? There is food in the kitchen which means, "Ah!" Many of our discovery moments took place over cookies, popcorn, or other delightful snack moments.

Next I realized we needed a term that DeWayne could relate too. That brought meaning to him to draw him into the calm to help redirect and focus him. Hence the term "Our Central Command Post": **Our** - for our home kitchen, **Central** - because the kitchen tends to be the central focus in many homes bringing comfort; and **Command Post** - draws in the military lingo bringing comfort of his military life to his family life.

Our next steps needed to include techniques that included all the family. TBI and PTSD are family matters that require family healing. Our kitchen was extremely old and needed remodeling. I took this opportunity to sit down with a cabinet maker to discuss possibilities.

We covered what needs had to be met, and he let us know what he would be able to do. I then took my ideas to DeWayne's Occupational Therapist where we could cover more in-depth what we needed to create at home. This process took several months of communication.

The final plans still required some fine-tuning as the cabinet maker became very involved in our family needs. Over time, he would learn more, and return with suggestions he saw that could be possible. Collaboration between many made Our Central Command Post possible. The final product has been a blessing. Our new kitchen cabinets allow for flexibility to meet our family dynamics -- not just My Love's needs. Which was the true goal.

Kitchen Calendar with Plexiglass and Sticky Notes.

Plexiglass inlay with whiteboard tape and dry erase markers. Over the years we have learned the top of the cabinet is valuable to have important phone numbers. Middle section is for DeWayne, he is most successful with no more than three tasks a day.

Bottom left hand section we write in dinner ideas. The bottom right hand section came in later when we realized that DeWayne was getting upset at our daughter without understanding why. We soon discovered it was because he couldn't remember what her schedule or chores were. It was time to create a section to support him in being a DAD! This also supported Addy in being a daughter - it was harder for her to pull a fast one on daddy.

This set up truly allows us to keep each other accountable as well as just keeping all our important information very easy to access.

Kitchen Calendar to Track Daily Activities

Reflection Point

Use the notes pages in this book to think through the key points of each chapter.

- What systems can you implement in your home that would eliminate stress for all members of the house?

- What would you need to purchase to make it happen?

Notes

_____

_____

_____

_____

_____

_____

_____

_____

_____

_____

_____

_____

_____

_____

_____

_____

_____

_____

_____

_____

_____

CH 4: HOW DRY ERASE MARKERS SAVED
OUR MILITARY FAMILY

Every day I look at my husband and I am happily reminded of how lucky I am that he was able to come home to me ... to all of us!

Even as we live through the new normal, his presence is a gift. Another gift I never imagined would have such an impact are the dry erase markers we keep in the house.

We have dry erase markers of every color and style gracing our kitchen for the Plexiglas cabinet door and my "Mom calendar."

I love the colors.

The colors help keep things fresh, bright and cheerful. Dry erase markers are easy to clean off, to change, to brighten up a day.

They are just so fun and add a touch of spice to our lives. The colors are also fun to draw pictures with, which our daughter's friends have blessed us with the drawing of flowers, smiley faces and words of encouragement.

You might be asking, "where did we get the idea for these dry erase markers?" Well let me tell you: we received them as the best wedding gift from an amazing friend - little did we know that God was working his magic for many years down the road in so many ways.

The note that came with the dry erase markers simply stated, "these are to leave love notes on your bathroom mirror for each other often". A few years after DeWayne came home from Iraq our dry erase markers disappeared from our bathroom only to appear in our daughter's bathroom.

Our daughter liked our mirror notes so much that she knew it was time to draw on hers too, so we purchased a set for her bathroom. Addy's bathroom is the main one for the home, so when guests come over, they also leave messages or works of art on the mirror. Dry erase markers officially transformed from being a family thing to being a Village thing, helping raise and support a family.

We are a family who will continually need support. We will always be asking for help of some kind. When guests come over and leave cheerful messages or drawings - to us - this means they are a part of this family. They are accepting of our every changing daily new normal. It brings comfort and joy.

Dry erase markers have brought stability into our ever changing daily new normal of a life. They have been a part of bringing peace, joy, and continual love. To this day, dry erase markers are truly the best wedding gift we received.

Reflection Point
Time to reflect on the chapter:

- What are some ideas that are simple to do, but bring joy into your home?

- What would you need to purchase to make it happen?

Notes

CH 5: HIDE-N-SEEK

As a kid, playing hide-n-seek was a blast. However, when you become an adult, it can take on a not-so-pleasant meaning.

When you're walking out the door and realize the keys to the truck are missing or when my husband is raging through the house because his wallet isn't where he thought he left it, hide-n-seek isn't so much fun. It took many times of playing hide-n-seek before we found a tracking device for those commonly misplaced items.

The round key tracker you see in this photo was worth it. Systems save our sanity.

The tracking device had to be small enough to fit into his wallet, act as a keychain and link to my cell phone.

The final undoing was after spending an hour twice in one week searching for both sets of vehicle keys. I finally broke down and purchased the tracking system. Next step was to add to my daily task list of making sure all keys, his wallet, and sunglass case were properly stored in their set locations.

Yes, one more task to add to my ever-growing list of caregiving.

As much as it sucks sometimes, having sanity in our family is worth it. This task soon became a routine, and I haven't given it much of a second thought since our new system is in place.

Reflection Point
Use the notes pages in this book to think through the key points of the chapter.

- Is there something in your day-to-day routine that drives you crazy?

- Is there a process or system you can put in place that will fix the issue?

Notes

_____

_____

_____

_____

_____

_____

_____

_____

_____

_____

_____

_____

_____

_____

_____

_____

_____

_____

_____

_____

_____

_____

_____

_____

_____

_____

_____

CH 6: MEDICATION TIME:
SYSTEMS SAVED US AGAIN...

There are many options out there to help someone take their medication on time and correctly. Some are simple pill boxes to using timers.

The key to making daily medicine-taking a routine process and less stressful is discovering what works best in your home, for your care recipient, but that takes time. For us, this was another lengthy process.

My Love's Occupational Therapist spent many dedicated hours for a couple years teaching DeWayne how to fill his medication box and set timers in his phone all so he would take the correct medications at the correct times. Following a minor accident in the home along with a medicines mishap, we finally decided, sadly, that this was too overwhelming for DeWayne. It was time for me to take this task over to manage.

After trial and error, we finally realized that to support DeWayne's success, we could only have his medication for ONE day out on the counter.

Even for me, trying to remember what medications were to be taken when, and reading each medication bottle was tiresome. I needed to create yet another system that supported my duties of filling his medications.

First, I bought a second and third medication box so I could fill three weeks at time. Filling weekly was too much.

Second, I wrote down a daily schedule of his medications, name, amount, what it was for and when he was to take it. This got my brain rolling. I remembered from my ambulance days how stressful it was not only for the patient, but for us as the first responders, trying to figure out what medications a person had taken and when.

So the editing of DeWayne's medication list began.

It was time to start keeping track of medical conditions, surgeries, dates, emergency contact people, service dog info, and so on.

Then where do we keep copies of this medical list? Sounds simple, right? Well, it wasn't.

I tried keeping a copy in DeWayne's wallet. He kept taking it out. So I keep a copy in my purse, in his service dog's vest, with our vehicle's insurance paperwork, in the bucket of medications, in the kitchen cabinet and email a copy to his emergency contact people.

When the ambulance arrives I hand them a copy of the medical list to keep. They greatly appreciate this list. In turn they hand it over to the ER who also benefits from the medical list.

Sweet love notes and an organized medicine system helps us avoid very dangerous dosing mistakes. The next two photos are examples of documents we keep on hand for emergencies in the case that we need to relay information quickly but don't have time to write it down. These sheets stay updated and kept in easy to locate places.

VA Medical Center Name, Address, Phone #. Primary Care Doctor & Team (Silver Team)

Veteran's Name & Last four   **Service Dog: Name, Breed, Sex**
Address
City, State, Zip
Home#   Cell#

Spouse or Caregiver's Contact info – Home # & Cell #
Holds full power of attorney (If you hold any legal documents for care.)
Other emergency contact people, (recommend to list at least 2 alternates just in case)

List of Main Medical Issues
Traumatic Brain Injury
Post-Traumatic Stress Disorder
Bi-Lateral Hearing Loss
Fall Risk
Silent Seizures
Un Explained Tremors
Allergy to: PCN

Medication List:

Morning 7am-9am
1 ½ - Escitalopram Qxalate 20MG Tablet (for depression)
1 – Docusate NA 50mg Sennosides 8.6mg TAB (constipation)
1 – Tolterodine Tartrate 4MG SA TAB (frequency of urination)
1 – Levothyroxine NA 0.137mg tab (synthroid) takes with full glass of water (Hashimoto's thyroiditis)
1 – Acetaminophen 500mg tab

12 NOON Take with you
1 – Acetaminophen 500mg tab

Evening 5pm
1 – Rosuvastatin CA 80MG TAB w/dinner (for high Cholesterol) (limit use of grapefruit)
1 – Acetaminophen 500mg tab

Bed 8pm – 10pm
1 – Prazosin HCL 5mg cap (for nightmares)
6 - Divalproex 500mg 24HR (ER) SA TAB (for mood, silent seizures, migraines)

As needed
Ketoconazole 2% cream, Apply 2x a day (as needed for skin fungus)
Ketoconazole 2% shampoo, Apply every 3rd day to scalp, chest, & arms (as needed for skin fungus)

Last Update May 5, 2017

FRONT SIDE

THIS PAGE IS FOR LISTING IN DETAILS MEDICAL ISSUES

ANY ASSETIVE DEVICES THAT ARE USED

SURGERY DATES AND WHAT TO INCLUDE OUTCOMES

*Tires easily: with TBI, most of his sleep is recovery and requires 8 to 10 hours of sleep nightly with naps almost daily and at least an hour of down time daily
*Short term memory
*Easily lost, confused, disoriented
*At times doesn't understand what is being said to him and what he says in return doesn't make sense
*Bi-lateral hearing loss
*Migraines/headaches
*Silent Seizures: headache, blood shot eyes, glossy glanced over eyes, stutters or slurred speech, non-responsive, then requires several hours of sleep to recover. Silent seizures a person doesn't move, their body basically freezes up.

*He is wear sunglasses when outside at all times and avoid direct sunlight for long periods of time.
    *Wears sunglasses inside when lights are too bright and bothersome

**He is good with his hands – when his tremors are under control and his concentration is intact.
*He is upbeat and happy normally – except when he has overdone himself
*He enjoys life and is grateful to have a second chance

** Service Dog through **
Name: Registration No:
Breed: Gender: Spayed:
Vaccinations Dates: *Rabies Vaccination Date:*
Distemper Adenovirus   *Producer ZOE*
Para-Influenza - Parvovirus   *3yr LIC/Vacc*
Borderttella Bronchiseptica Becterin

BACK SIDE

Reflection Point
Your new normal may include medication schedules.

- Are you a caregiver for someone who needs specific prescriptions administered at specific times of day?

- The notes section on the next page is for listing out all of the medications and then you can start sorting out the details from there. It can seem like a lot, but YOU CAN DO IT!

Notes

_____
_____
_____
_____
_____
_____
_____
_____
_____
_____
_____
_____
_____
_____
_____
_____
_____
_____
_____
_____
_____
_____

CH 7: STICKY NOTES ARE LITTLE SQUARES OF JOY

Centralization of our chaos didn't stop in the kitchen. We had to create support throughout the house. Sticky notes are amazing. They come in so many shapes, colors, and sizes -- perfect with a family's ever-changing new normal.

Communication after My Love's return home wasn't easy. All three of us had to learn to share information in new ways.

Addy was only six years old when her Daddy came home from Iraq, so she was still learning how to successfully communicate with others in general. DeWayne had to learn how to communicate all over again, and the two of them were a perfect match. Looking back, I was the one who had to work hardest. I had to learn how to communicate with a man who has a TBI while teaching a youngster with a good old fashion German temper to talk instead yelling. I wasn't a good referee.

Once I realized this, I knew it was time to share a new experience together, as a family.

We started out using the large-sized sticky notes while sitting at the table in Our Central Command Post and wrote down how to talk to each other. We started out with simple communication skills, as each person wrote down what they needed to do to effectively: listen, speak, control anger/disagreements. I always knew when it was time to rework these sticky notes because I would be the referee from work over the phone.

Sticky notes also came in handy for me personally. I would write affirmations throughout the house - this too shall pass - remember to breathe first - you are a strong person - messages that were encouraging as well as supportive.

We soon discovered that we could leave messages for each other. Addy would draw pictures. Love notes started appearing. Joy was starting to find its way back into our home.

Smiles and Laughter are free when you create a road map that allows them to be there.

To this day, we have sticky notes strategically placed throughout our home in support of DeWayne's ever-changing, daily new normal. Some light switches now have duct tape on them (for the sensor porch light) with a sticky note stating, "This light is to stay on."

**Sticky notes reminding My Love that it is okay to forget,
but it is not ok to be mean about it.**

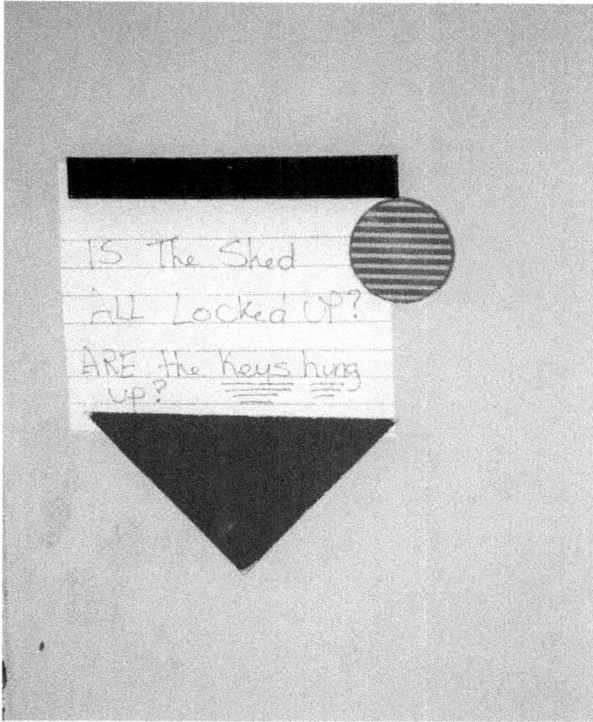

Sticky notes with messages reminding us
to make sure the shed is locked and key hung up.

Best part is, when the message needs to change
it is simple to change the sticky note.

Reflection Point

Use the notes pages in this book to think through the key points of the chapter.

- Can you think of ways that sticky notes could help you and / or your family or family member?

Notes

CH 8: SIMPLICITY CAN COME
IN THE FORM OF A TRASHCAN

When simply thinking about the concept of "simplicity" as it pertains to my life -- it causes me to giggle. Not too many years ago, simplicity and my name in the same sentence would have never gone together. In fact, my sister would have a few giggles with me over the complexity of my life!

Then, a life-altering event changed not only my life, but also the lives of my family members.

Living with a spouse who has a traumatic brain injury (TBI), Post Traumatic Stress Disorder (PTSD), and chronic pain due to spinal issues, we have learned to live with the ever-changing daily "new normal" with touches of strange humor.

Here we are, 12 years post-deployment, still learning the value of simplicity. We still work on what to simplify and when. One of my favorite discoveries is the elevated trashcan.

Who would have thought raising the trashcan up and placing empty bags on the side would make our lives more simplified?

First off, we raised the trashcan up in support of my husband's aim. In all honesty, none of us have claim to fame in the world of trashcan basketball, but there are some unique benefits to our newfound trashcan discovery.

More trash makes it into the trashcan than on the floor, with the added bonus of less trash slime sliding down the wall. The elevated trashcan also makes taking out the trash much easier for my husband. The elevation doesn't require him to bend over, so he is able to take it out himself. Now the only issue is having the trash taken out before it reaches maximum overload, a.k.a. exceeding weight limits, for hubby's help taking the trash out.

Not only did elevating the trashcan give us some wonderful benefits - we went a step further and placed spare bags on the sides of the trashcan.

Sounds simple, right? Exactly.

This simple step encourages speedier replacement of the trash bag into the empty trashcan. As moms everywhere can attest, there is nothing worse than going to throw away trash only to discover a bare naked trashcan.

Simplicity isn't always easy to figure out when you live with an ever-changing daily new normal.

Once you have mastered something that works one day, it may become a national disaster the next day. The only things we can do are hope for the best, always keep trying, and never give up. For as my grandmother always said, "Hope is an action word, now make it happen!"

Something as simple as putting extra bags and raising the height of the trash can makes a big difference.

Reflection Point

You may not need to change your trash can but there may be other things that you could do to make your home more adaptable to your loved one. If you can't think of anything, keep an eye on your loved one to see if they struggle with anything that you may not have noticed before. Sometimes is the little things that seem simple to us, but can improve to make life easier for them.

Notes

CH 9: AVA, OUR NEWEST SUPERHERO

Ava, the service dog, came into our lives Thanksgiving 2015 and changed our lives forever. Be prepared, having a service dog takes over your world.

Although they are very helpful, they require a lot of attention, continual training, consistency -- basically a routine -- which is a challenge when living with an ever-changing daily new normal of "TBI Man"!

Ava has been a blessing not only for DeWayne but also for the family. She has brought comfort and joy that was needed. Best of all, she has brought the support DeWayne needed to feel he could breathe some again. He no longer holds on to me so tight that he leaves marks on my hands or arms when in public. It is still a challenge to get him out of the house but Ava, "The Superdog," is here to save the day!

A surprise discovery with Ava came about one night.

The organization that awarded Ava to DeWayne requires Ava sleep in a kennel at night. Several times a week, Ava would start pawing at her kennel while making a noise, just like talking, not quite a barking sound.

I soon realized she was trying to get to DeWayne because he was having his violent dream enactments. Ava was responding to DeWayne's distress. Thankful to my handy construction brother-in-law, we designed a bed for Ava that took her out of her kennel and put right next to DeWayne where she was needed most! Now at night when DeWayne's dream enactments take over, Ava, The Super Dog, comes to the rescue by laying on top of him or getting in between us.

The weight of her body, the nudging of her nose wakes him up gently. I am thankful he responds so well to her because he never did to me. I am also thankful to have less attacks on me in the middle of the night.

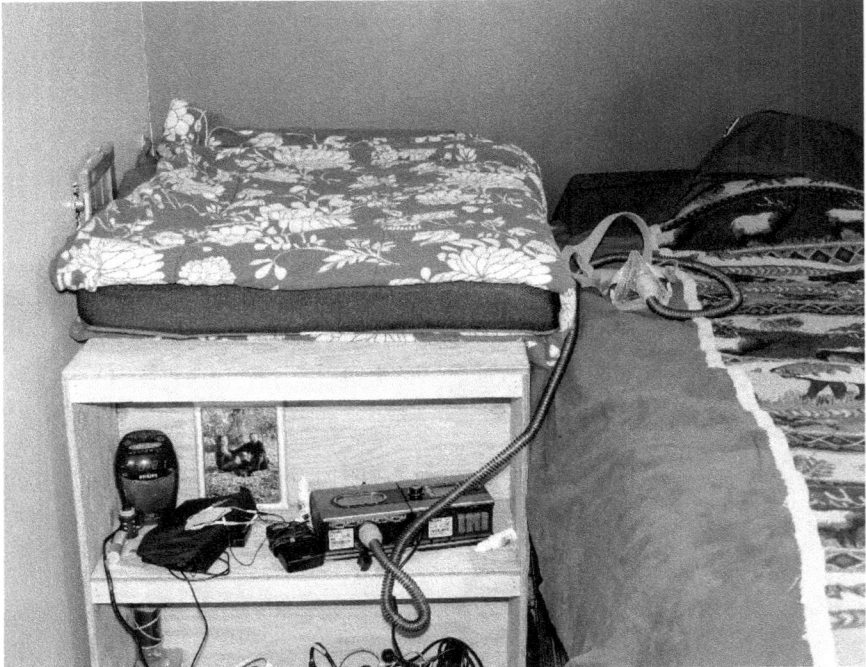

Ava's bed is right next to ours so at night she can help when we need her.

Reflection Point

If a service animal seems like a great way to help your loved one, make sure to check out the "Resources" section of this book. There are incredible resources for service members who think a service dog would benefit them. Remember, as a caregiver, you may also benefit by having a furry friend. Sometimes we caregivers have anxiety and stress too. For us, Ava helped the whole family, which was a fun surprise.

Notes

CH 10: HOT FEET -- A METAPHOR FOR CAREGIVERS

I don't know about you, but as a kid, I could walk around all day in the summer without my shoes on. The hot southern New Mexico sun beating down on the clay ground, the goat heads, and hot rocks created a tough combination to walk on.

It would drive my parents crazy, but I would persevere.

Over the past few years, I have realized walking from my home to the trash-bin without shoes on isn't as comfortable as it used to be. I live in Idaho now where the sun isn't as hot. My tough, callused feet have become very tender.

How do tough feet relate to being caregiver in an adaptive home? Easy.

In the beginning we feel we can take on the world while still having plenty of time to breathe. Laundry is done, kitchen clean, dinner cooked, kids off to school with lunches, groceries bought and put away all while getting that nice shower, clean clothes on, fixing the hair, and makeup done. Along with tending to the medical needs of our care recipient 24/7. We are true superheroes in our own little worlds at home.

Or at least that is what we are telling ourselves.

We have to "fake it until we make it." It's what we are supposed to do. (Just like writing this section of the book in the truck while my husband is at a veteran's golf clinic) we overcome and adapt. Just like our shoeless feet as kids -- we grow calluses to continue giving care to our care recipients, but calluses break down over time. Many of our care recipients can tell you

43

stories about calluses on the children's feet in Iraq. How they would break down.

Of course caregivers know there is help out there.

We know and understand we need to ask for help.

We know and understand we can't do it all.

We know and understand there are limitations to our overcoming and adapting.

We know and understand we are the makers of our own caregiver burnout.

What we don't know is that our true supporters will always be there helping if we just say what we need help with!

Here is a where I started to realize my calluses were starting to wear off.

Through counseling, I have accepted that there are days I need help with preparing meals. Those days are usually when we are at the VA. Our beautiful Super Dog Ava, causes us to leave roughly an hour and half before his appointment to give us time to drive. Preparation to leave requires getting both service dog and husband in the car with everything needed for the day, wallet, sunglasses, extra water, lunch, and snacks. Appointments can last an entire day, to which many military families can attest.

Next, is the challenge of finding of parking spot.

There are times I have to take a chance dropping DeWayne off near a location close to an entrance, while strategically locating a potty spot for Ava, then go park a mile away and pray when I walk back that DeWayne is where I left him. Other times we are lucky to find closer parking. Then we take Ava potty, put on her uniform and walk to the VA medical center. It is always a trek from the parking to the VA which is a slow pace for DeWayne.

Once we get that figured out, we've got to navigate the inside of the VA medical center to get him to his appointment location. Sounds easy? Well, it's not.

Just like Ava, DeWayne also needs a potty stop prior to his appointment. Our "VA days" are well-mapped out, planned as much as possible, because they create high stress mentally and physically for both of us. This has nothing to do with the VA having poor quality care, but because I have to keep DeWayne on track. I need to constantly remind him why we are at the VA, which doctor appointments are next, what the doctor said, and why we are going to the next location for extra added testing.

I like that our providers try to schedule in same-day testing to keep us from going back multiple times in a week. It does cause for longer days but at least we are done when we go home. There are days we spend 4-6 hours inside the VA medical center walls. These long days challenge me to adapt and overcome.

VA Day calluses have begun to wear down. Why is it so hard to admit I need help?

That is a great question. For me, it comes from a fear of failure: fear of failing my family, fear of what others will think of me, fear of placing more pressure on our daughter to pick up my slack. Sometimes I even fear that I'm not good enough to be my husband's spouse or caregiver. These all may seem silly, but they are many caregiver's realities. We have to learn to overcome our own self doubts. For most of us, we have been tossed into this caregiver role with little to no preparation. We have learned along the way to meet the needs of our care recipient and to work our own needs into daily living as well.

Caregivers need to learn to reach out to the world around us to show others we are here, and educate people on what we do and why. Many times, all we have to do is explain, and the public is ready to step in to assist. We are the Hidden Heroes supporting our American Heroes because we choose to be, we want to be, and because we love it.

As a caregiver, we have to find ways to support our care recipient the best we can. This support not only helps them be more successful each day, it takes some of the daily burden of being a caregiver off of us. For many of us, being a caregiver is going to be a long-term normal lifestyle that we slowly grow into. We are going need to find ways to support ourselves internally. A fellow caregiver once told me, "We're the sucking wound of the church, we'll always be the family in need." But with a supportive caregiver community, you don't have to do it alone -- nor feel like a "sucking wound".

To prevent caregiver burnout, you need a plan for an adaptive home, permission to ask for help, personal time for self-care, and confidence that you are moving forward by pursuing your best.

All these ideas shared with you are flexible/adaptive to your personal needs. When you live in a home that needs to be adaptable to an ever-changing, daily new normal you need to find ways to help your solid structure flex. I hope you have found some strategies you can adapt to fit your needs. My wish for you is to learn to thrive in your own ways, find strength in numbers for you are not alone.

For We are a Military Family who is American Made! We Reach Higher, Dream Brighter, and Hold on Tighter.

Reflection Point

Reflecting on being a caregiver and what that means for you and your family's new normal.

- What causes you the most stress about caregiving?

- What helps you unwind from stress?

- Who can you call when you need to talk?

- Who can you call when you need help in an emergency?

Notes

_____

_____

_____

_____

_____

_____

_____

_____

_____

_____

_____

_____

_____

_____

_____

_____

_____

_____

_____

_____

_____

_____

_____

_____

ABOUT THE AUTHOR

Jeannette Davidson-Mayer is the author of her first book Our Central Command Post. She holds a degree in business management with an emphasis in human resources. She also has a background as an emergency medical technician.

Jeannette is the Board Secretary for R4 Alliance along with being one of the founding members of the Alliance. Jeannette is the proud mom of a daughter entering college. Addy wants to work on a degree in Military Family Mental health, a topic close to her heart. Jeannette is the primary caregiver to DeWayne, her husband of 13 years. Her husband served in U.S. Army, then in the Army National Guard, where he deployed to Iraq in Operation Iraqi Freedom 2004/2005.

He lives with TBI, PTSD, bilateral hearing loss, spinal column issues, and many complications related to these medical conditions. Jeannette is serving as Idaho's Elizabeth Dole Fellow Class of 2016. She advocates for fellow Hidden Heroes and firmly believes a collective voice creates power. That the support caregivers give each other provides strength for many to keep moving forward. As with so many caregivers, self-care is necessary and Jeannette has found hers in the gym five days a week in the early morning hours. She also enjoys sharing her story through writing and public speaking.

RESOURCES

R4 Alliance, www.R4Alliance.org - Our membership provides programs of excellence that support Recreation, Specialized, as well as Support services. This allows R4 to have impact across the veteran community and ensure networking of a variety of skills to address veteran needs.

Elizabeth Dole Foundation, www.elizabethdolefoundation.org - Our Vision is an America where military caregivers are empowered, appreciated, and recognized for their service to our nation.

Bob Woodruff Foundation. www.bobwoodrufffoundation.org - We invest in positive returns. Positive returns for the veterans returning to their families and communities and positive returns for every dollar donated to their long-term wellbeing. It is by connecting communities with the brave heroes returning to them, that we are best able to provide more than stopgap measures, but long-term solutions that take a holistic approach to recovery. The Bob Woodruff Foundation stands out from the sea of 46,000 nonprofits that serve veterans by the way in which we find, fund and shape innovative programs within that maze.

Military Veteran and Caregiver Network, www.milvetcaregivernetwork.org - The Military and Veteran Caregiver Peer Support Network (MVCN) offers peer-based support and services to connect those providing care to service members and veterans living with wounds, illnesses and/or injuries. The Network is modeled on the nationally recognized, evidence-based programs of the Tragedy Assistance Program for Survivors (TAPS), which has provided compassionate peer-based support to more than 60,000 loved ones of those who have died during their service in the Armed Forces. The mission of the MVCN (together with our partners) is to provide our nation's pre- and post-9/11-era military and veteran caregivers with peer support to reduce their isolation and increase their senses of connectedness, engagement, hopefulness, wellness, as well as their knowledge and skills.

Operation Family Caregiver, www.operationfamilycaregiver.org - Operation Family Caregiver coaches the families of returning service members and veterans to manage the difficulties they face when they come home. OFC is a personalized program, tailored specifically to the struggles of each family. Through proven methods, the program teaches military families how best to navigate their challenges, resulting in stronger and healthier families.

Operation Family Caregiver is a program of the Rosalynn Carter Institute for Caregiving (RCI). RCI supports caregivers – both family and professional – through advocacy, education, research and service. It establishes local, state, national and international partnerships committed to building quality, long-term home and community-based services.

www.ingramcontent.com/pod-product-compliance
Lightning Source LLC
Chambersburg PA
CBHW060557100426
42742CB00013B/2593